WOLVES

A Book of Postcards by Tim Fitzharris

FIREFLY BOOKS

A FIREFLY BOOK

Photography © 1999 Tim Fitzharris
Produced by Terrapin Books, Santa Fe, New Mexico
Project Manager: Joy Fitzharris

ISBN. 1-55209-419-7

Published in Canada in 1999 by
Firefly Books Ltd.
3680 Victoria Park Avenue
Willowdale, Ontario
Canada M2H 3K1

Published in the United States in 1999 by
Firefly Books (U.S.) Inc.
P.O. Box 1338, Ellicott Station
Buffalo, New York
USA 14205

Printed in Hong Kong

Gray Wolf

PUBLISHED BY FIREFLY BOOKS • WILLOWDALE, ONTARIO, CANADA

Gray Wolf and Pup

PUBLISHED BY FIREFLY BOOKS • WILLOWDALE, ONTARIO, CANADA

Postage

Photography © 1999 Tim Fitzharris

Gray Wolf Howling

PUBLISHED BY FIREFLY BOOKS • WILLOWDALE, ONTARIO, CANADA

Gray Wolf Pups

Postage

PUBLISHED BY FIREFLY BOOKS • WILLOWDALE, ONTARIO, CANADA

Gray Wolf

Postage

PUBLISHED BY FIREFLY BOOKS • WILLOWDALE, ONTARIO, CANADA

Gray Wolf and Pup

Postage

PUBLISHED BY FIREFLY BOOKS • WILLOWDALE, ONTARIO, CANADA

Gray Wolf

PUBLISHED BY FIREFLY BOOKS • WILLOWDALE, ONTARIO, CANADA

Photography © 1999 Tim Fitzharris

Gray Wolf

PUBLISHED BY FIREFLY BOOKS • WILLOWDALE, ONTARIO, CANADA

Gray Wolves at Deer Carcass

PUBLISHED BY FIREFLY BOOKS • WILLOWDALE, ONTARIO, CANADA

Postage

Gray Wolves

Postage

PUBLISHED BY FIREFLY BOOKS • WILLOWDALE, ONTARIO, CANADA

Gray Wolf Pup

PUBLISHED BY FIREFLY BOOKS • WILLOWDALE, ONTARIO, CANADA

Gray Wolf

PUBLISHED BY FIREFLY BOOKS • WILLOWDALE, ONTARIO, CANADA

Postage

Gray Wolf

PUBLISHED BY FIREFLY BOOKS • WILLOWDALE, ONTARIO, CANADA

Gray Wolf with Pup

Postage

PUBLISHED BY FIREFLY BOOKS • WILLOWDALE, ONTARIO, CANADA

Gray Wolves

Postage

PUBLISHED BY FIREFLY BOOKS • WILLOWDALE, ONTARIO, CANADA

Gray Wolf

PUBLISHED BY FIREFLY BOOKS • WILLOWDALE, ONTARIO, CANADA

Gray Wolf

Postage

PUBLISHED BY FIREFLY BOOKS • WILLOWDALE, ONTARIO, CANADA

Gray Wolves

PUBLISHED BY FIREFLY BOOKS • WILLOWDALE, ONTARIO, CANADA

Gray Wolves

PUBLISHED BY FIREFLY BOOKS • WILLOWDALE, ONTARIO, CANADA

Postage

Gray Wolf

Postage

PUBLISHED BY FIREFLY BOOKS • WILLOWDALE, ONTARIO, CANADA

Gray Wolves at Deer Carcass

PUBLISHED BY FIREFLY BOOKS • WILLOWDALE, ONTARIO, CANADA

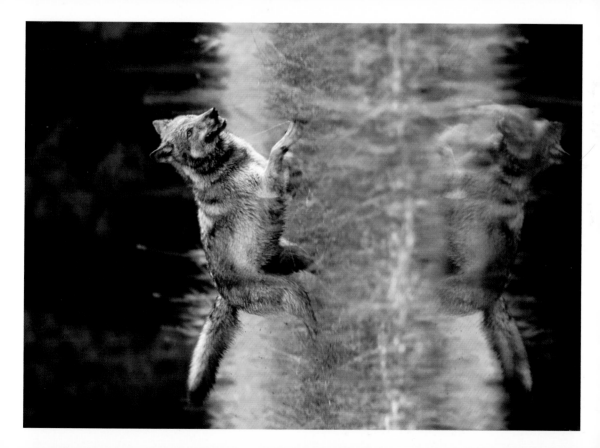

Gray Wolf

Postage

PUBLISHED BY FIREFLY BOOKS • WILLOWDALE, ONTARIO, CANADA

Gray Wolf

PUBLISHED BY FIREFLY BOOKS • WILLOWDALE, ONTARIO, CANADA